FROM TOY TO ICON
How Barbie Shaped Generations Of Girls

TRISHA KIM

Table of contents

Chapter 1

Introduction

Barbie has been a subject of widespread discussion for her representation of femininity, gender roles, and body image. However, her journey from a toy to an icon has also opened up important conversations about women's empowerment, self-discovery, and the challenges they face in society.

The movie "Greta Gerwig's Barbie" has further highlighted these themes and encouraged both men and women to defy gender norms and societal expectations. By acknowledging the impact Barbie has had on shaping the perceptions of femininity and beauty for young girls, we can continue to have constructive conversations around gender representation and body image.

A doll with blonde hair, blue eyes, and complete make-up named Barbara Millicent Roberts has been a part of our lives since the 1960s. She is a doll from the imaginary town of Willows, Wisconsin, and she has blue eyes and blonde hair.

Margaret Roberts and George Roberts have five children, and she is the eldest of the five (or maybe six) children they have. Does her name seem familiar to you? Ruth Handler, an American entrepreneur, has developed her "Barbie" throughout the years. She has worn dozens of outfits and has had a variety of jobs, ranging from a cashier at McDonald's to an astronaut. Her "Barbie" has been influenced by world-renowned labels such as Donna Karan, Christian Dior, and Givenchy. In 1965, four years before the first man stepped on the moon, Barbie was even used to depict the female space cadet.

For a long time, Barbie has been an indispensable toy for young girls. She comes with everything a young girl could want, including her ideal home, dress, accessories, and, of course, her renowned lover, Ken. You can get Barbie character curtains, bedding, and even home décor in Turkey. You can even find them in Turkey.

Mattel, the company that makes the doll that is worshiped, recently extended its "Fashionista" line by introducing three new Barbie dolls. This expansion took place five days ago. In addition to having a variety of skin tones, eye colors, hairstyles, fashionable attire, and even flat feet, these dolls come in a range of sizes in addition to being tall, curvaceous, and tiny.

According to Evelyn Mazzocco, the senior vice president and worldwide general manager of the Barbie empire, "Barbie has always offered girls choices: from 180 career options and the inspirational roles she represents to her endless fashion options and accessories." Barbie has long been recognized for providing girls with a wide range of alternatives. From a business viewpoint, this current action by Mattel is an effort to stimulate sales of the renowned doll, which have dropped in recent years. From a social standpoint, however, the growth of Barbie - a global and cultural symbol being distributed in 150 nations worldwide - reveals much more.

First emerging in a black-and-white striped bikini, Barbie has epitomized beauty and fashion for decades. In 1965, the American Girl Barbie reached the market, complete with a bob hairdo. Later, in 1971, Live Action Barbie joined the ranks on shop shelves sporting a hippy headband. This doll has even run for president six times since 1992, appearing in a royal blue skirt, blazer, high-heeled shoes, and a string of pearls, with her hair perfectly coiffed exquisitely.

Mattel has not confined itself to tinkering with numerous varieties of Barbie's outfits and her face, either. In 1980, the brand created Black Barbie, including an afro. That same year, a Hispanic Barbie was produced, called Teresa.

Mattel has made enormous attempts to bear in mind the shifting societal norms when developing the Blonde Bombshell. Despite its popularity, the doll has also garnered criticism for its small waist and physically impossible body proportions. Several studies have pointed to the adverse consequences Barbie has on young girls, stressing the negative influence the doll has on the body image and self-esteem of small girls.

The tests also found that the dolls might have long-term consequences on female psychology as well, perhaps prompting girls to develop eating problems. Indeed, an online poll done by Yahoo Health, published last month, indicates that the majority of young females in the U.S. are dissatisfied with their looks and have negative body image. Of the females questioned, 94 percent stated they feel embarrassed of their bodies. This report reveals why Barbie's unrealistic image creates a concern for young girls.

The development of Barbie is also intimately related to the ideals of beauty that have also shifted throughout the years. Unrealistic beauty standards take a major toll on women mentally, while the young girls who are affected by supermodels and Barbie dolls aspire to acquire an unhealthy body size. In the 1950s, Marilyn Monroe became the gold standard for beauty among women and girls in the U.S. with her voluptuous physique. Monroe's body mass index (BMI) was 19.1 - greater than the BMIs of today's supermodels.

A decade later, flat-chested women like English actress and model, Twiggy, started to dominate beauty trends. Later, American actress Farrah Fawcett, supermodel Cindy Crawford, and Victoria's Secret model Heidi Klum - one of the world's highest-paid models - became beauty symbols. The ideal norm for beauty finally transformed into the image of the stick-thin lady. The present criteria are more or less the same for Turkish girls and women who have adored thin models in recent years, even if the curvy woman is also a dominating type.

"The compelling fact is that, just as women have started to make dramatic gains in the areas of education, employment, and politics, the ideal female body began to look like a malnourished, prepubescent girl, one who is weak, emaciated and non-threatening, women were increasingly encouraged to discipline their bodies through diet and exercise to conform to ideals that were almost impossible to achieve," states the Bradley University's Body Project which aims to increase the awareness of the female body in all sizes and shapes.

Maybe the absence of a "socially conscious" Barbie is one of the reasons for the reduction in Mattel's earnings. "Barbie mirrors the world girls perceive around them. Her capacity to change and grow with the times, while keeping true to her soul, is essential to why Barbie is the number one fashion doll in the world," said Mattel President and CEO Richard Dickson, highlighting the doll's importance on girls.

Chapter 2

Who is Ruth Handler?

Ruth Handler (November 4, 1916–April 27, 2002) was an American inventor who designed the renowned Barbie doll in 1959 (the doll was named after Handler's daughter Barbara). Barbie was debuted to the world at the American Toy Fair in New York City. The Ken doll was named after Handler's son and was presented two years after Barbie debuted. Handler was the co-founder of Mattel, a firm that makes a range of popular toys.

Handler was born Ruth Marianna Mosko on November 4, 1916, in Denver, Colorado. Her parents were Jacob and Ida Mosko. She married Elliot Handler, her high school lover, in 1938.

With Harold "Matt" Matson, Elliot developed a garage workshop in 1945. Their firm name "Mattel" was a combination of the letters of their surname and first names. Matson eventually sold his stake in the firm, so the Handlers, Ruth and Elliot, acquired complete control. Mattel's earliest products were picture frames. However, Elliot finally began building miniature furniture from picture frame leftovers. That proved to be such a success that Mattel moved to create nothing but toys. Mattel's first big-seller was the "Uke-a-doodle," a toy ukulele. It was the first in a series of musical toys.

In 1948, the Mattel Corporation was legally formed in California. In 1955, the business transformed toy marketing forever by securing the rights to make the iconic "Mickey Mouse Club" items. The cross-marketing push became normal practice for subsequent toy firms. In 1955, Mattel created a popular patented toy cap gun dubbed the burp gun.

In 1959, Ruth Handler designed the Barbie doll. Handler would eventually refer to herself as "Barbie's mom."

Handler saw her daughter Barbara and pals playing with paper dolls. The youngsters utilized them to play make-believe, picturing positions as college students, cheerleaders, and adults with occupations. Handler aimed to design a doll that would better assist the way young girls were playing with their dolls.

Handler and Mattel unveiled Barbie, the adolescent fashion model, to apprehensive toy shoppers at the annual Toy Fair in New York on March 9, 1959. The new doll was significantly unlike the baby and toddler dolls that were popular at the time. This was a doll with an adult body.

What was the inspiration? During a family trip to Switzerland, Handler noticed the German-made Bild Lilli doll at a Swiss boutique and purchased one. The Bild Lilli doll was a collector's piece and not meant for sale to children; yet, Handler used it as the foundation for her design for Barbie. The Barbie doll's first lover, the Ken Doll, appeared two years after Barbie in 1961.

New 'Ken' Doll Puzzles A Boy

Handler said Barbie was a symbol of freedom and promise for young girls and women:

"Barbie has always represented that a woman has choices. Even in her early years, Barbie did not have to settle for merely being Ken's lover or an obsessive shopper.

She had the clothing, for example, to establish a career as a nurse, a stewardess, and a nightclub singer. I think the possibilities Barbie symbolizes helped the doll catch on early, not only with daughters—who would one day make up the first significant wave of women in management and professionals—but also with mothers."

The Story of Barbie

Handler built a personal tale for the very first Barbie doll. She was called Barbie Millicent Roberts and she was from Willows, Wisconsin. Barbie was a teenage fashion model. Now, however, the doll has been manufactured in several variations associated with over 125 different vocations, including the president of the United States.

Barbie appeared as either a brunette or blond and in 1961, a red-headed Barbie was created. In 1980, the first African-American Barbie and Hispanic Barbie were created.

The first Barbie was sold for $3. Additional apparel based on the newest runway styles from Paris was available as well for between $1 and $5. In 1959, the year Barbie was debuted, 300,000 Barbie dolls were sold. Today, a pristine condition "#1" Barbie doll may bring as much as $27,000. So far, more than 70 fashion designers have designed outfits for Mattel, utilizing more than 105 million yards of fabric.

There has been significant disagreement regarding Barbie's figure ever since it was recognized that if the doll were a real person, her dimensions would be inconceivable 36-18-38. Barbie's "real" dimensions are 5 inches (bust), 3 1/4 inches (waist), and 5 3/16 inches (hips). Her weight is 7 ¼ ounces, and her height is 11.5 inches.

In 1965, Barbie had flexible legs and eyes that opened and shut. In 1967, a Twist 'N Turn Barbie was produced that featured a moveable body that twisted at the waist.

The best-selling Barbie doll of all time was the Totally Hair Barbie of 1992, which had hair from the top of her head to her toes.

Amid suspicions of false financial reporting, Handler resigned as Mattel's president in 1973. She and her husband ended up quitting the firm completely in 1975, Handler was charged on charges of fraud and false reporting to the Securities and Exchange Commission in 1978, to which she pleaded no contest. As a consequence, she was sentenced to 2,500 hours of community service and a $57,000 fine, Biography.com reported.

She subsequently stated her breast cancer diagnosis in 1970 left her "unfocused" regarding Mattel's restructuring at the time, ultimately leading to her departure, citing The Guardian.

After beating breast cancer and suffering a mastectomy in 1970, Handler researched the market for a suitable prosthetic breast. Disappointed by the alternatives available, she went about constructing a replacement breast that was more comparable to a natural one. In 1975, Handler secured a patent for Nearly Me, a prosthesis constructed of material near in weight and density to those of real breasts.

Death
Handler suffered colon cancer in her 80s. She died on April 27, 2002, at the age of 85. Handler was survived by her husband, who died on July 21, 2011.

Legacy Handler founded one of the world's most successful toy businesses, Mattel. Her Barbie doll is one of the most famous and iconic toys in the world. In 2016, the

Museum of Decorative Arts in Paris hosted a Barbie display including hundreds of dolls with artworks inspired by Barbie.

Chapter 3

Barbie through the years

Hop aboard the pink time machine, as we transport you away to the captivating 20th century, when the brilliant Ruth Handler stood at the intersection of invention and creativity. One courageous move beyond the ordinary led her to construct a legacy that would resonate through time itself. In this riveting age, when the world was cocooned in the ordinary, Handler unfurled her visionary soul, spawning the renowned Barbie doll - read on as we explore into the amazing real tale behind it.

Greta Gerwig's feminist rendition of the Barbie doll has won worldwide praise at the movie office. While we're aware of the doll's roots as a product of the Mattel toy corporation, the mind behind the invention and the birth of the Barbie doll typically remains lesser-known.

The Big Barbie Doll Debut and Its True Story

Ruth Handler and her husband, Elliott Handler, gave the world to the renowned Barbie doll in 1959. Before this milestone, as detailed by the LA Times, Handler had worked as a secretary at Paramount Studios. In a destined turn of events, she nourished her husband's enthusiasm for manufacturing plastic giftware, including clocks, bowls, mirrors, and more, which rapidly grew into their thriving company. Their odyssey unfolded, ultimately leading to the development of the popular Barbie doll.

A symphony of elegance, empowerment, and bold flair, the moniker "Barbie" soon grew to become an anthem for change, and a symbol that would forever be inscribed into the very fabric of worldwide pop culture. A pink revolution, carved in plastic and welded in fantasies has come to reality.

Ruth Handler's Inspiration Behind the Barbie Doll

Barbara, Handler's daughter, served as the inspiration for Barbie's conception when Handler witnessed her playing with paper dolls. Driven by a desire to encourage youngsters to envisage their future ambitions, she tried to innovate beyond the usual plastic baby dolls of the period. Drawing inspiration from a realistic female doll she met in Germany, she set out to offer a new degree of realism to her concept for Barbie. It was this spark of imagination that seeded the seeds for what would soon become a worldwide phenomenon.

Barbie Doll Ruth Handler's real tale

Barbie's first doll, named the 'Barbie Teen-Age Fashion Model,' debuted at the American Toy Fair in 1959. Donning a trendy black-and-white striped bikini, combined with elegant black high heels, she donned cosmetics, and a ponytail, and carried a USD 3 price tag. She was a huge success, with 350,000 dolls flying off the shelves in the first year alone!

This represented only the beginning of Barbie's adventure, going from a model into an astronaut, doctor, and teacher. The arrival of "Ken" in 1961, Barbie's dashing companion, significantly broadened her story. In 1969, the Christie doll, an African American companion of Barbie, surfaced, but the first black Barbie doll made her formal entrance in 1981.

Beyond the Toybox

Barbie transcends basic playthings to become a cultural icon. Her impact reached pop culture, literature, and even music. The captivating "Barbie Girl" by the famous band Aqua, caught the spirit of her magnetism, resonating over radio waves and dance floors. Barbie's style spawned trends in fashion too, encouraging generations to emulate her famous feminine image.

The Barbie mania increased demand for limited editions and antique dolls, while arguments about her beautiful image generated worries about beauty expectations and self-esteem. Detractors questioned body image and norms, raising questions about their influence on young minds. Soon, the progression towards inclusion inspired re-evaluation, prompting the Barbie brand to adapt and produce dolls representing a varied society.

Barbie Shapes Dreams for Generations

From her roots in a California garage to her omnipresence in playrooms throughout the globe, Barbie's journey is a monument to Ruth Handler's vibrant vision of empowerment! Barbie encouraged young minds to dream of endless worlds and tales still untold. Today, as Xboxes and iPads have many hooked, the famous doll continues to make its way into kids' playrooms. And as for adults? It still invokes nostalgia, guts, and elegance.

In the great scheme of cultural icons, Barbie stands for dreaming, dedication, and creativity. As the world progresses, she stays a treasured companion on the road of development, defying conventions, and embracing the dynamic spirit of generations past, present, and future.

Barbie's spectacular ascent continued, and Mattel launched accessories like the Barbie Dream home, sports vehicles, and additional apparel. Next came additional dolls including Barbie's closest friend, Midge, and younger sister, Skipper. Starting in 1968, Barbie incorporated dolls from diverse races, starting with the Black Christie doll.

Barbie is nearing her 65th year. She has altered in looks throughout the years and has had hundreds of occupations ranging from pilot to politician. Some commend her for helping women break over the glass barrier, while others blame Barbie for sexualizing girls and encouraging unrealistic body types.

In the early 2000s, Barbie struggled to remain relevant as rival toy producers started making dolls with greater variety. In 2020, Mattel unveiled its most diverse doll line ever as Barbie fought to redefine herself. Nobody can argue Barbie's appeal; she is one of the top-selling toys of all time.

Chapter 4

Evolution of Barbie in Society: From Idealisation To Empowerment

In the ever-evolving world of play, one toy has remained supreme since the 50's — the Barbie doll. A symbol of beauty, prosperity, and femininity, Barbie has molded the lives of small girls worldwide.

Growing up in the 90's the variety of Barbie's you could get your hands on was bountiful and a surefire method to earn yourself the fame Barbie herself would be proud of. Malibu Barbie, Ballet Barbie, Stable Set Barbie equipped with Nibbles the horse who immediately befriended your My Little Ponies. But amid the strewn floors and boxes was missing arguably the most sought-after Barbie of them — Greta's Barbie.

The recent release of the live-action Barbie film, directed by feminist visionary Greta Gerwig, promises to reinterpret this lasting doll's legacy. Known for her true-to-life inner workings of the feminine psyche in her flicks Ladybird, Frances Ha, and most famously her version of Little Women. Greta's deep investigation of feminine ambitions, dreams, and disarrays makes her more than equipped for the duty of personifying the doll that small girls project their fantasies.

As we look into the psychology underlying Barbie's popularity and her developing effect on young brains, we unearth a complicated relationship between play, development, and cultural standards.

Barbie Play

Play is a crucial component of childhood, it acts as a cornerstone for development and learning. Through diverse games and toys, youngsters explore, learn rules, and construct narratives about the world around them. With Barbie's pervasive presence, she plays a vital part in this process.

When we delve into the psychology of child development mixed with the ideals inherent inside popular toys we can see the enormous influence they have on influencing children's perspective of the world.

Dolls such as Barbie, become windows through which youngsters discover societal conventions, values, and beliefs. We all know the ages of 3-7 are the 'formative years', as they build the basis for our cognitive development and shape personality characteristics.

The Doll That Touches Hearts And Minds

Research at Cardiff University's Centre for Human Developmental Science evaluated the influence of doll play on children's cognition using neuroimaging equipment. They revealed that even solitary doll play engaged children's areas for empathy and social processing, underscoring the relevance of dolls in promoting emotional intelligence.

Barbie's influence goes beyond emotional development, including cognitive schemas and identity construction. Schemas, mental symbols that organize information, are influenced not just by personal experiences but also by societal influences, including music, TV, and in this instance, toys.

With Barbie presented as the symbol of female beauty and prosperity, considerable discussion has been ignited concerning idealized femininity. While Mattel views Barbie as inspiring, opponents claim her image fosters unattainable expectations and outdated gender roles.

The Barbie Effect

The "Barbie Effect" has attracted attention for its devastating repercussions. Research reveals that exposure to Barbie idealism might alter physical ideals, discrimination, and professional goals.

The unattainable beauty standards embodied by Barbie create an allure that fuels young girls' desire for a body type linked to success and popularity but also one of the very unhealthy standards when Barbie's unattainable measurements, if translated to reality, would render her physically incapable of menstruating.

This influence has frequently resulted in a separation between those who conform to her image and those who do not, possibly leading to feelings of alienation and diminished self-esteem.

However, recent studies show that broadening Barbie's body types, such as adding tall, voluptuous, and petite dolls and a range of races might lead to more accurate self-perception and build a feeling of inclusion.

Shaping Society's Beauty

Barbie may be considered much like the Kardashians, as contemporary influencers that hold enormous effect on macro social ideals of beauty, success, and femininity as well as individual self-perception.

Her representation might encourage people to adopt her beliefs and aesthetics, impacting their tastes. The overwhelming popularity of Barbie multiplies her effect, making her a potent force in molding generations' identities.

A new study has dug into the influence of the Barbie Effect on young girls' conceptions of professional achievement. An intriguing research at Oregon University studied the jobs young girls felt they might follow after engaging with several dolls - a conventional Barbie, a Doctor Barbie, or Mrs Potato Head. The findings yielded some unbelievably sad insights; showing girls who engaged with either the traditional Barbie or the Doctor Barbie expressed confidence in their ability to pursue only half the number of careers they perceived boys could, whereas those who interacted with Mrs Potato Head believed could aspire to an equal number of professions as the boys in the study.

The Future Of Barbie

Recognizing the harmful effects, Mattel, Barbie's maker, has made efforts to address concerns. Over the past 15 years, Barbie has grown to encompass varied body shapes, vocations, and racial representations. A recent study reveals that these adjustments significantly improve self-esteem and inclusion, enabling females to identify with more realistic versions of the doll.

While tremendous success has been made in diversifying Barbie, the influence of these alterations on young brains is still developing. Gen Alpha, growing up with these new dolls, could have more favorable schemas compared to their predecessors which would generally impact society's ideas of femininity.

The new live-action Barbie film by Greta Gerwig offers the potential to reinvent Barbie's position in girls' lives. With Gerwig's feminist outlook, the film may dismantle conventional beliefs and give a sarcastic take on women.

In many respects, Barbie's path mimics our socioeconomic growth. From an icon of unrealistic dreams to an emblem of diversity and empowerment, Barbie's evolution mirrors our evolving beliefs and ambitions.

As we go ahead, it is vital to grasp the psychological complexities at play and continue leading this famous doll toward a future that inspires and empowers the generations to follow.

Within the social and political turmoil of the 1960s and 1970s, Barbie's image, and the conversation around her portrayal, acquired form and altered. If young girls grow up witnessing the image of Barbie, they are ideally taught that beauty is having a slender figure, blonde hair, and blue eyes. "As a doll with which young girls could emulate an ideal womanhood, Barbie quickly became an object of cultural criticism". The conversation surrounding her position was generally recognized as having a considerable impact on American history. The ideal body image has always played a key influence in the early years. Around the time the Barbie doll reached the market, the feminist movement was blossoming. Women did not want to be bound and constrained inside a given function, which throws forward issues on Barbie's durability. How did Barbie 'survive' this societal transformation with the idea that her marketing image restricts Barbie to a narrow variety of identities? The doll's regularity of shifting depiction has substantially benefited its longevity. However, society's body image demands never totally faded. Discourse lasted throughout the 20th century, leaving its influence on today's society.

So, how has Barbie altered throughout time to preserve the interests of a larger audience, and how has this effort benefited her in obtaining an iconic status? Mattel Company suffered years of criticism and struggled to raise sales since Barbie's appearance did not match her broad audience. In the year 2016, a fashion designer incorporated plus-size models in his presentation during New York Fashion Week. That same year, with the advent of beauty assuming all forms and sizes, toy manufacturing firm Mattel chose to unveil a range of ethnically diverse dolls containing three new body types, seven skin tones, twenty-two eye colors, and twenty-four hairstyles. The notion of these dolls is surrounded by rhetoric that lends Barbie a feeling of personality, which was built up by her ethnic buyers. She was able to appeal to new customers since her look altered.

Appearing in similarity to the young children who played with the doll, gave Barbie a new, realistic persona. Her sense of personhood is shown by the multiple dimensions of her social identity, such as her new ethnically diversified look.

Though Barbie continued to evolve through societal changes and disclose new layers of her personality, there was a paucity of promotion for these new dolls. Most folks were not even aware of the new doll. Perhaps Mattel meant for this result? Considering it was a major risk to launch these new dolls, it is extremely probable that they were envisioned to be neglected. Even if the new product failed to affect customers favorably, it still goes to demonstrate how radically our social environment has evolved over the years. This was the first time we saw changes to the assumption that women need to be skinny to be attractive. "It was a society that made Barbie – literally and figuratively. Her universe was intended to grow, like ours" (BillyBoy, 1987). More and more individuals are breaking the molds of cultural expectations while exhibiting self-confidence. We have grown more welcoming of various shapes and sizes.

American beauty norms have altered considerably because individuals are more prone to be affected by the media. With some still sustaining the slender image, others are drifting away from this mindset. In 2007, the program 'Keeping Up with the Kardashians' aired its inaugural episode. We observed their figures onscreen that ignored the iconic Barbie look. The media switched to idolizing curvy forms such as Kim Kardashian West, Beyoncé, and Christina Hendricks. Their outfits have become iconic now and are propelling a movement that advocates body acceptance.

So, would this be the end for Barbie dolls because we have new cultural icons in the media? Considering Barbie is known to adapt and alter to suit cultural norms, it is predicted that Mattel will adhere to these existing views. Predictably, Mattel produced a range of celebrity Barbie dolls that include musicians, actresses, and even sports, who all have a prominent presence in current culture. Some resemble the looks of Beyoncé, Nicki Minaj, and even Diana Ross. Mattel had plans to remain current and celebrate modern and historical role models. Unfortunately for Kardashian fans, they still have yet to appear in a series of Barbie dolls. However, I just read on Twitter that Kim Kardashian West has her prototype from Mattel. Even if we have changed norms, some celebrities still seem to support Barbie dolls. Kylie Jenner, a huge influencer in the media, recently changed into a real-life Barbie doll for Halloween. Needless to say, Barbie continues to remain current over the 60 years of her life.

Barbie has without a doubt influenced countless lives and is considered a cultural icon. The historical history of Barbie offers a dialogue that casts a light on what Barbie tells about our society. It illustrates where we have come from, where we are, and where we are headed in terms of the social environment. Barbie reinforced the unreasonable ideals of what women should look like. Even though our culture now is much more welcoming and celebrates different body kinds, the impacts of the doll still linger, and I don't believe we will ever be able to escape it.

It was intriguing for me to research this issue. As it has played a part in my life, it has also made its impact on society for six decades, and I feel that Barbie will stay in current culture for many more years to come. She hasn't failed to remain current since she is continually changing and growing to fit with society. I presume her contentious identity and depiction will continue to develop. The ideas of Barbie undergo a conflictual and communal process of deliberation among the social variables affecting the doll, the buyer, and the designer. In whichever manner you choose to view and interpret the nature of Barbie, it is considered that her nature is that of a continually renovated object, that has disclosed evidence about social life as a whole.

Chapter 5

Inspiring Young Minds and Unlocking Limitless Potential

In a world filled with unlimited possibilities, Barbie stands tall as an iconic character who has inspired generations of young girls.

Far beyond simply a doll, Barbie symbolizes empowerment, inventiveness, and the boundless potential that lives inside every kid. In this interesting blog, I investigate why Barbie is not simply a toy but a catalyst for growth, creativity, and the development of vital life skills.

Today, Barbie dolls come in diverse skin tones, body types, and hairstyles, enabling young girls to see themselves represented and honoring the individuality of every person. Barbie promotes the virtues of acceptance, empathy, and appreciation of diversity, building a more inclusive and understanding society.

Imagination Unleashed:

Barbie awakens the flame of creativity in young brains like no other. With her vast selection of vocations, from astronaut to veterinarian, Barbie inspires girls to dream big and believe in their potential. Through creative play, girls may step into diverse roles, explore alternative professions, and create a feeling of curiosity and ambition that will move them ahead in life.

Promoting Diversity and Inclusion:

Barbie has undergone a tremendous change to represent the beauty of variety. Today, Barbie dolls come in diverse skin tones, body types, and hairstyles, enabling young girls to see themselves represented and honoring the individuality of every person. Barbie promotes the virtues of acceptance, empathy, and appreciation of diversity, building a more inclusive and understanding society.

Encouraging Self-Expression:

Barbie's vast assortment of outfits and accessories helps young girls to express their personalities and establish their particular style. Through dressing up their dolls, kids learn about colors, patterns, and creative combinations, fostering a sense of self-expression and encouraging them to accept their unique likes and preferences.

Building Social and Emotional Skills:

Playing with Barbie dolls may help young girls acquire key social and emotional skills. As they participate in pretend play and develop creative situations, kids learn about problem-solving, empathy, and teamwork. Through narrative and role-playing, students manage emotions, form connections, and strengthen their communication skills, creating a firm basis for good social interactions in the future.

Empowering Girls to Dream Big:

Barbie has been an advocate for empowering females to overcome obstacles and achieve their aspirations. Through the "You Can Be Anything" tagline, Barbie inspires girls to believe in themselves and conquer whatever hurdles they may encounter. By displaying strong, successful female role models, Barbie instills the concept that there are no boundaries to what girls may achieve, pushing them to accept difficulties and strive for success.

Barbie goes beyond the realm of a simple toy, becoming a symbol of strength, creativity, and inspiration for young girls worldwide.

From nurturing creativity and self-expression to supporting diversity and building vital life skills, Barbie has a tremendous influence on the development and maturation of young brains.

So, let's celebrate the ongoing legacy of Barbie and the various ways she continues to inspire generations, reminding us all that with persistence, dreams can come true and every girl can be whatever she wishes.

Chapter 6

The Barbie movie's revolutionary effect on society

There is no question Greta Gerwig's Barbie grabbed the globe by storm. Although on the surface it seems like a humorous movie about the famous Barbie doll, it is much more. With themes of feminism, female empowerment, and the quest for self-discovery, Barbie has become highly relevant to women worldwide.

"Barbie found out who she was, and I went through a period in my life where I didn't know where I was," said Kristen Francis, a junior education major at UNC Asheville.

The movie underlined the message the Barbie doll has been promoting for decades: that women can perform the same tasks men can do, as well as be in positions of authority.

Senior environmental studies major Gaby Shenot emphasized the significance of representation in the movie.

"I am a stem major, so I think having a lot of those careers being highlighted in the movie was important and inspiring," Shenot said.

However, to some Barbie has grown more contentious because of its portrayal of international concerns, particularly the numerous challenges women confront.

"The second Barbie got into the real world she was immediately objectified. That connected with me," said Cady Stanton, an aspiring art major at UNCA.

The movie also highlights the patriarchy in our culture, and how it affects both men and women.

"The movie gave a really clear idea of how easy it is for men to think they can come in and take over," Shenot remarked. "I think it did a good job highlighting the fact that the patriarchy's still an issue we have to face every day."

Many may consider Barbie "anti-men," given its representation of toxic masculinity. However, it is an honest picture of males being victims of the patriarchy, along with women. It pushes guys to rethink their masculinity.

"We're all going through our similar gender stereotypes and the patriarchy doesn't even work toward men," added Stanton. "The patriarchy doesn't work for anybody, and I feel like that was the point."

Men have come to better comprehend women's challenges in society because of the movie's influence. According to a poll done by Resume Builder, 53% of viewers said Barbie boosted their perception of women in the workplace. two in three respondents claimed Barbie made them more conscious of patriarchy in the workplace.

"I think there has been a bit of a bigger movement for men to understand where women are coming from when we speak against the patriarchy," said Shenot.

Barbie has awakened the eyes of males, presenting the truth of how women are treated in society. Essentially, the stereotyped roles of women and men in society are flipped in the movie.

"I thought it was interesting how the movie portrayed the difference between Barbie World and the real world and how it sucks for women," said Dylan Mayo, a freshman at UNCA. "Watching it, I felt like I was kind of the problem."

Barbie encourages both men and women to defy gender norms and society's expectations of who they should be.

www.ingramcontent.com/pod-product-compliance
Lightning Source LLC
Chambersburg PA
CBHW071002290526
45795CB00005B/1756